T0345854

Ethics and Politics in
Tagore, Coetzee and
Certain Scenes of Teaching

Other Titles in the Series

Social Science across Disciplines is a
new series that brings to a general audience
a selection from the papers and lectures
delivered at the Centre for Studies in
Social Sciences, Calcutta (CSSSC), over
the last four decades. They fall into two
categories—first, a selection from among
the Occasional Papers circulated by the
Centre's faculty, and second, from the two
series of memorial lectures in the name of
Sakharam Ganesh Deuskar (for lectures on
Indian History and Culture) and of Romesh
Chunder Dutt (for lectures on Political
Economy).

Gayatri Chakravorty Spivak

Ethics and Politics in Tagore, Coetzee and Certain Scenes of Teaching

Introduction by
Anirban Das

Centre for Studies
in Social Sciences, Calcutta

OXFORD
UNIVERSITY PRESS

OXFORD
UNIVERSITY PRESS

Oxford University Press is a department of the University of Oxford.
It furthers the University's objective of excellence in research, scholarship,
and education by publishing worldwide. Oxford is a registered trademark of
Oxford University Press in the UK and in certain other countries.

Published in India by
Oxford University Press
2/11 Ground Floor, Ansari Road, Daryaganj, New Delhi 110 002, India

First Edition published in 2019

ISBN-13 (print edition): 978-0-19-948669-4
ISBN-10 (print edition): 0-19-948669-7

ISBN-13 (eBook): 978-0-19-909540-7
ISBN-10 (eBook): 0-19-909540-X

Typeset in Berling LT Std 10/14
by Transtics Data Technologies, Kolkata 700 091
Printed in India by Replika Press Pvt. Ltd

Contents

Contents

About the Author

Gayatri Chakravorty Spivak, literary theorist and feminist critic, is University Professor of Humanities at Columbia University and founding member of its Institute for Comparative Literature and Society. Considered one of the most influential postcolonial intellectuals, Spivak is best known for her essay 'Can the Subaltern Speak?' and for her translation of and introduction to Jacques Derrida's *De la grammatologie*.

About the Editors

Partha Chatterjee is Professor of Anthropology and of Middle Eastern, South Asian and African Studies at Columbia University, New York, USA. A member of the CSSSC faculty for 36 years, he was also its Director from 1997 to 2007, and continues as Honorary Professor of Political Science. Among his books are *Nationalist Thought and the Colonial World* (1986), *The Nation and Its Fragments: Colonial and Postcolonial Histories* (1993), *A Princely Impostor? The Strange and Universal History of the Kumar of Bhawal* (2001), *The Politics of the Governed* (2004), and *The Black Hole of Empire* (2012).

Rosinka Chaudhuri is Director and Professor of Cultural Studies at the CSSSC. She is also the first Mellon Professor of the Global South at the University of Oxford. She has written *Gentlemen Poets in Colonial Bengal* (2002), *Freedom and Beef Steaks* (2012), and

The Literary Thing (2013) and edited *Derozio, Poet of India* (2008), *The Indian Postcolonial* (co-edited, 2010), *A History of Indian Poetry in English* (2016), and *An Acre of Green Grass and Other English Writings of Buddhadeva Bose* (2018). She has also translated and introduced *Rabindranath Tagore: Letters from a Young Poet* (2014).

About the Introduction Writer

Anirban Das is Associate Professor in Cultural Studies at the CSSSC. After graduating in Medicine, he shifted to an interdisciplinary space in the humanities and the social sciences with a PhD in Philosophy. He is interested in and has published essays on feminist theory, postcolonial theory, the body, science studies and medical epistemology, Marxian theory and 'theory' in a broad sense, and has edited the first comprehensive volume on deconstruction in Bangla (2007). His academic monograph *Toward a Politics of the (Im)Possible: The Body in Third World Feminisms* was published in 2010. He is currently working on three book projects and a number of essays.

General Introduction to the Series

Partha Chatterjee and *Rosinka Chaudhuri*

This series of publications from Oxford University Press brings to a general audience a selection of the papers and lectures delivered at the Centre for Studies in Social Sciences, Calcutta (CSSSC), over the last four decades. They fall into two categories: first, a chosen few from among the Occasional Papers circulated by the Centre's faculty and second, from the two series of memorial lectures in the name of Sakharam Ganesh Deuskar, for lectures on Indian history and culture, and Romesh Chunder Dutt, for lectures on political economy.

The CSSSC was founded in 1973 as an autonomous research institute financed primarily by the Indian Council for Social Science Research and the Government of West Bengal. Since then, the Centre, as it is ubiquitously known, has established an academic reputation that places it at the crest of research institutes of excellence in India. Its faculty works in the fields of history, political science, sociology, social anthropology, geography, economics, and cultural studies. Its unique interdisciplinary culture allows for collaborations between scholars from different fields of research that might not find support in traditional department-based institutions, attracting students and researchers from across the country and abroad.

The R.C. Dutt Lectures at the CSSSC have focused on themes from economic theory, economic history, and development policy, mostly relating to India. As is well known, Romesh Chunder Dutt (1848–1909) served in the Indian Civil Service from 1871 to 1897. On retirement, he lectured at the University of London, UK, and wrote his classic work in two volumes, *The Economic History of India under Early British Rule* (1902) and *The Economic History of India in the Victorian Age* (1904). He was elected president of the 1899 session of the Indian National Congress. Apart from his extensive writings on the colonial economy, the condition of the peasantry, famines, and land rights, Dutt was also a poet in English and a novelist in Bengali, writing on historical and social themes. Over the years, some of the most eminent economists of India have delivered the R.C. Dutt lectures at the Centre. Among them are Sukhamoy Chakrabarti, K.N. Raj, V.M. Dandekar, Ashok Rudra, Krishna Bharadwaj, A. Vaidyanathan, Suresh Tendulkar, Prabhat Patnaik, I.S. Gulati, Amit Bhaduri, C.T. Kurien, Praveen Visaria, Kaushik Basu, Geeta Sen, Debraj Ray, Abhijit V. Banerjee, Ravi Kanbur, and Dilip Mookerjee. The lectures selected for publication in the present series will capture key debates among Indian economists in the last four decades in topics such as the crisis of planning, economic liberalization, inequality, gender and development, sustainable growth, and the effects of globalization.

The S.G. Deuskar Lectures began as a series on Indian nationalism but widened to reflect the cross-disciplinary interests the CSSSC nurtured, featuring a range of distinguished speakers on the history, culture, politics, and society of India. Sakharam Ganesh Deuskar (1869–1912) was Maharashtrian by ancestry and member of a family that migrated in the mid-eighteenth century to the Santal Parganas on the border of Bihar and Bengal. A schoolteacher and journalist by profession, he is best known for his Bengali tract *Desher Katha* (1904)—a damning indictment of the exploitative and violent character of British colonial rule—which is reported to have sold 13,000 copies in five editions within five years during the Swadeshi movement in Bengal. Some of the finest scholars and artists of modern India have delivered the Deuskar Lectures, including, among historians, Ranajit Guha, Tapan Raychaudhuri, Irfan Habib, Satish Chandra, Romila Thapar, Partha Sarathi Gupta, Sabyasachi Bhattacharya, Sumit Sarkar, Dipesh Chakrabarty, Muzaffar Alam, Gyanendra Pandey, Sanjay Subrahmanyam, and Shahid Amin; among philosophers, J.N. Mohanty and Bimal Krishna Matilal; among artists and art critics, Geeta Kapur, Vivan Sundaram, K.G. Subramanyan, and Ghulam Mohammed Sheikh; among social theorists, Gayatri Chakravorty Spivak, Sudipta Kaviraj, and Veena Das. A selection of these lectures will now be reprinted in this current initiative from Oxford University Press.

Occasional Papers published by the CSSSC represent the research of the CSSSC faculty over the years. Many of these papers were later published in journals and books, some becoming classic essays that are essential reading for students and researchers in the field. Some of the most important works in the Indian social sciences, it would be fair to say, are represented here in the form of papers or drafts of book chapters. Of the nearly 200 Occasional Papers published so far, we will reprint in the present series only those that are not already in wide circulation as journal articles or book chapters. Included among our Occasional Papers will be the current initiative of the Archives Series Occasional Papers, meant specifically to showcase the collection in the CSSSC visual archives.

By turning these outstanding papers into little books that stand on their own, our series is not intended as a survey of disciplinary fields. Rather, the intention is to present to the reader within a concise format an intellectual encounter with some of the foremost practitioners in the field of humanities and social sciences in India. R.K. Narayan, in his childhood memoir, *My Days* (1947), had written that when, as young men, he and his friends had discussed starting a journal and were thinking of names for it, someone suggested 'Indian Thought'. 'There is no such thing' was the witty response from a friend. Narayan nevertheless began publishing *Indian Thought*, a quarterly of literature, philosophy, and culture, which lasted all of one year. We suggest that this series might, in the end, prove his friend wrong.

Introduction

Anirban Das

According to the first note to this essay, a version of the text was presented as a paper in Kolkata on 10 February 2003. This was the first day of the two-day S.G. Deuskar lecture delivered by Gayatri Chakravorty Spivak at the CSSSC. Fifteen years after that event, the essay still makes points expansive and important enough to retain contemporary relevance in multiple ways. Like many of Spivak's other pieces, the arguments move in a tortuous path—with perfect clarity, in spite of a few condensed articulations—that may need some elaborations to help navigate its course. Introducing a Spivak text is always a daunting task which, like the proverbial fools, only a few would undertake. What I try to do is to follow the overall movement of the arguments as I understand them, and put in an explanatory note here and there. I do not summarize the arguments. This introduction does not have a spoiler alert.

To begin with, as the title indicates in so many words, this is an essay on ethics and politics. It is, at the same moment, throughout infused with a concern to bring forward the way the literary works in the production of that ethics and politics. Of course, the notion of ethics operative here is far removed from an inventory of moral principles to be followed in action. To speak in relation to the pragmatic solutions to problems of behaviour, the ethical, here, is something like a much broader notion of a mentality or sensibility, which remains part of one's being. One has to remember that to express it in this manner is to go against the spirit of what is ethical in this sense. For, the expansive notion of the ethical put to work in the present context is an 'experience of the impossible', not reducible to a sensibility, or to a mentality. It indicates an opening out to the 'other' across an incommensurable divide. As the separation is, by definition, non-bridgeable, one cannot really reach beyond the divide. Yet the reaching out is an inalienable condition of one's being. Hence, the 'double bind' of bridging the unbridgeable. The ethical experience in this sense thus becomes the experience of the impossible.

To continue the line of reasoning, the ethical also escapes, while still being in relation with, the calculations of the political. Without these calculations, one cannot reach the limits towards the ethical; yet the latter does not thereby remain derivable from the former. On the contrary, the ethical, here, marks a break. The essay declares at the very beginning, the 'eruption of the ethical interrupts and postpones the epistemological' (p. 3). The phrase 'interrupts and postpones' is instructive. The break, inaugurated by the ethical in the epistemic endeavours to calculate and contain the other, is also a postponement, an act of deferral of (full) presence. It is not a negation of those calculations but a postponement of their attaining full presence in the form of a successful and satiated containment of the other. To refer back to Spivak's earlier and famous formulation in a form of intertextuality, this is something like the mode of acceptance of responsibility to politically represent the other whom one cannot represent ontologically. The risk of (even a) political representation is in a circumscription of the other's ontology (reducing them to one's own language). Yet that act is unavoidable. The work of the ethical is in interrupting and rendering ever incomplete this act of epistemic colonization. This epistemic colonization is not only a colonization in the domain of knowledge but something that is an inseparable part of any knowledge process: the making of the other as object. At the end of this introduction, we will expand upon the ways in which the literary enacts the ethical. Before that, let us follow some of the insights into the working of the literary which Spivak articulates and instantiates in the essay.

At a certain point, the text speaks about the task of the literary intellectual 'to restore reference boringly in order that intertextuality may function; and to create intertextuality as well' (p. 10). Here, the reference is to the way one 'literary academic' (presumably the author, but the argument does not change if it is not) suggests the connection to Mozart's *Don Giovanni* in a choreography staged in a New York café. The link would, probably, have been missed by the audience otherwise. The notion of intertextuality, as against more pedestrian 'similarity' or 'difference', brings out associations on the basis of words, situations, metaphors, narratives, or any other trope at work. It may undermine or underline themes working in more than one text, on the basis of resemblances or oppositions. In this essay, Spivak 'creates' the intertextuality between J.M. Coetzee's novel *Disgrace* (2000) and Rabindranath Tagore's poem 'Apoman' (1910). The close association between the texts is highlighted through the call in 'Apoman' (Spivak calls it 'a dark poem') 'to be equal in disgrace' (p. 11) with those whom one has flung down, *Apomane hote hobe tahader shobar shoman* (p. 8). For, those who are below will 'bind you down there', *Jare tumi niche phelo she tomare bandhibe je niche* (p. 11).

Spivak is aware of the diverse ways in which this sharing of disgrace happens in the two very different texts. She writes about this difference in meticulous detail. Yet the responsibility to reach out to the other that constitutes an ethical move comes out clearly in her readings.

The ethical gesture—unlike the epistemic drive to calculate and contain the other—tries to build a relationship to the incalculable. This attempt cannot, thereby, consist in the setting up of instructions based on verifiable linear causalities. The work of the literary operates differently:

> The literary text gives rhetorical signals to the reader, which leads to activating the readerly imagination.... These are not the ways of expository prose.... Metaphor leans on concept and concept on metaphor, logic nestles in rhetoric, but they are not the same and one cannot be effaced in the other. (p. 18)

The work of the reader who learns to follow the logic nestling in rhetoric may touch, in her imagination, the ethical gesture. The task of the literary academic, in this sense, is in helping the reader to learn through her own attempts to follow the nuances of a text. Towards the end of the essay, Spivak elaborates on how a work of literary reading may bring out the importance of the ethical in thinking about what constitutes education in certain 'scenes of teaching'. The critique operating in fiction acts through the production of figures in certain ways, not by providing blueprints for unmediated social policy. One should remember, the opposition between the literary and the social sciences at work in these formulations are more in the register of thematics, not reducible to classification on the basis of given texts. Thus, the same text may be amenable to literary and social scientific readings, or may indeed call for both types of readings to be at work simultaneously. What is contrary is at the same moment complementary.

The signals that *Disgrace* is seen to send to the reader is constituted through one central trope and a number of intertexts being followed in the essay. One such intertextuality is between Lucy and Cordelia in *Disgrace* and *King Lear*, respectively. The father–daughter relationship between Lear and Cordelia begins with the word 'nothing' from Cordelia. Lucy's words with her father ends with '… perhaps that is a good point to start from again…. To start at ground level. With nothing. Not with nothing but. With nothing. No cards, no weapons, no property, no rights, no dignity' (quoted in the text, p. 11). Not going into the details of Spivak's extremely rich and nuanced reading of texts, I point cursorily at the differences between these two 'nothing(s)'. Cordelia both refuses the casting of love in value form (the question 'how much') *and* accepts it when she refers to the love for the husband being denied if the 'whole' of love is declared to be for the father. The economy of love and 'dynastic succession' constitute the import of Cordelia's 'nothing'. For Lucy, the 'nothing' is the immeasurable pre-originary non-presence that is impossible and scary at the same moment. Her gesture is, for Spivak, also a refusal to accept 'the affective value system attached to reproductive heteronormativity' (p. 15). Lucy does not accept her rape, she refuses the values which constitute rape and points at the impossibility of a successful undoing of wrongs through formal calculations. To be equal in disgrace is to reach out (impossibly) to a nothingness. This nothingness is not a withholding of response that occurs in death, in terror, through suicide bombing, the text underlines. Of course, one has to remember, literary figures do not embody given political or ethical positions. They send signals through acts of reading which disfigure them. Learning from the figures of Cordelia or Lucy happens through displacements.

The figure of Herculine Barbin ('the nineteenth century hermaphrodite who committed suicide but left a memoir, which Foucault edited and made available', p. 22) is placed beside Lucy to point at the 'rational kernel of the institution of marriage' (p. 22).

The concept-metaphors of rape, reproduction, generational continuity, the power axis between the man and the woman, all are played out in the spaces of marriage and family. In that space, the subaltern cannot yet speak to the political. As Spivak refers to her canonical article, her own attempts to hear the speech of the woman who speaks through her death is an ethical move but does not qualify as 'listening' by the political subject. This erstwhile subject lacks the institutionally valid apparatus to listen and hence cannot constitute itself as the subject. Similarly, the inscrutability of Lucy's gesture of reaching out to the other escapes the institutional calculus of Lurie, her father, or of a reading that tries to find an epistemically obvious agency.

That takes us to the figure of Lurie and the intertext with Kafka's *The Trial*. The phrase 'like a dog' links the two texts. In *The Trial*, the phrase indicates shame, a continuity of shame at the 'end of civil society' (p. 18). For Spivak, this is the way Lurie (as well as a certain reading of the text) misreads Lucy's response. The stress here is on the break in civility that perpetuates shame. For Lucy, on the other hand, this indicates a beginning from 'nothing', a sharing of disgrace. Interestingly, the way the text focuses on the opposite of what the intertext points at is through the making of the connection between the two. You establish a connection to something symmetrically opposed to what you suggest and hence emphasize the import of what you imply. In the movement of the text itself, Spivak talks about the trope—we mentioned earlier—of 'counterfocalization' at work.

The manifest focus of *Disgrace* is on Lurie, the father. As Lurie continues to misread Lucy's words and acts (already discussed earlier), for Spivak, the active reader gets the rhetorical signal to focalize on Lucy (p. 18). Lucy's attempts to imagine the other who is irreducible to the self, to put herself in the place of the other, get emphasized in the text through this work of counterfocalization, by moving through and beyond Lurie's calculations which are 'unable to touch either the gendered or the racial other' (p. 20). The ethical move is underlined in its difference from the calculus of civil society, a difference that is constitutive in the sense that the moves through that social are the necessary prequels to the touch of the ethical.

At the end of the text, we reach instances of learning from the other that the literary may give access to in unique ways. This mode of learning is itself an ethical gesture that is indissolubly linked to teaching. If, to educate the other, democratically, is also to learn from the other, then what does this learning consist of? Spivak describes, analytically, how teaching fails in multiple registers across gradients of power—rewritings of textbooks, 'sympathetic' questionings that remain oblivious in nuanced ways to the chasm separating the teacher and the student—to reach instances of silence (that a particular mode of education structurally produces, not being reducible to a question of intentions or expertise) in the scene of education. She also speaks of one instance of an effort that probably did elicit a fleeting and mild response, through acts of opening up to the text in painstaking detail, in which the teacher had been trying to reach the 'nothing' in which the receiver was inserted. This might have been an attempt to touch the disgrace which could make them equal. Avowedly, this was different from a large scale change in the politics of education:

> The number of calculative moves to be made and sustained in the political sphere, with the deflecting and overdetermined calculus of the vicissitudes of gendered class-mobility

factored in at every stop, in order for
the irony-shared-from-below communication
to be sustained at this level, would require
immense systemic change. (pp. 35–6)

In terms of an education that made a
permanent change, this was probably a failed
effort, having produced only a flicker of a
transient response. Yet the immensity of the
political change remains a greater failure if
inattentive to this flicker. The literary critic
might help us in being responsive, to learn
from 'the singular and the unverifiable' event,
generalizing but 'not on evidentiary ground[s]'
(p. 20). Spivak's own account here is also of
the nature of what she calls a setting to work
rather than that of an explication on the basis
of examples.

These are general points, generalizations
involving the need to attend to singularities.
Spivak's text is feminist and has important
things to say in the domain of the postcolonial.
In this introduction, we have not talked much
about those aspects. For, neither feminism nor
the postcolonial are regional issues ghettoed
out of the universals. These constitute
significant interventions in the field of theory
in general. The text in question, as also
Gayatri Chakravorty Spivak's oeuvre, repeats

the point in different articulations. Moving through theoretical reason's efforts towards a hermeneutic of suspicion regarding the 'I', and the political that tries to organize the field of suspicion (about the fixity of the subject) into game theory and rational choice parameters (p. 4), Spivak—following Lévinas—reaches the need for the interruptions that the ethical may enact in this organization. I leave the reader to share the text's training in literary imagination, acceding to the ethical in unique ways—and hence act out the impossible performative of the self in relation to the other.

Ethics and Politics in Tagore, Coetzee and Certain Scenes of Teaching

GAYATRI CHAKRAVORTY SPIVAK

Ethics and Politics in Tagore, Coetzee and Certain Scenes of Teaching[1]

Gayatri Chakravorty Spivak

It is practically persuasive that the eruption of the ethical interrupts and postpones the epistemological—the undertaking to construct the other as object of knowledge, an undertaking never to be given up. Lévinas is the generic name associated with such a position. This beautiful passage from *Otherwise than Being* lays it out, although neither interruption nor postponement is mentioned. That connection is made by Derrida.[2]

Here, then, is Lévinas for whom Kant's critical perspectivization of the subject and the rigorous limits of pure theoretical reason seem to have been displaced by the structuralist hermeneutics of suspicion. For Lévinas, structuralism did not attend to what in Kant was the mechanism that interrupted the constrained and rigorous workings of pure reason: 'The interests that Kant discovered in theoretical reason itself, he subordinated to practical reason, become mere reason. It is just these interests that are contested by structuralism, which is perhaps to be defined by the primacy of theoretical reason'.[3]

The relationship between the postponement of the epistemological in Lévinas and the subordination of pure reason in Kant is a rich theme, beyond the scope of this lecture. Let us return to what Lévinas will perceive as a general contemporary hermeneutics of suspicion, related to the primacy of theoretical reason: 'The suspicion engendered by psychoanalysis, sociology and politics weigh on human identity such that we never know to whom we are speaking and what we are dealing with when we build our ideas on the basis of the human fact'.[4] The political calculus thematizes this suspicion into an entire code of strategy defined as varieties of game theory and rational choice. This can be verified across cultural difference, backwards through history, and in today's global academic discourse. Over against this Lévinas posits the ethical with astonishing humility: 'but we do not need this knowledge in the relationship in which the other is the one next to me [*le prochain*]'.

Kant thought that the ethical commonality of being (*gemeines Wesen*—repeatedly mistranslated as 'the ethical state') cannot form the basis of a state. Surprisingly, there is a clear line from the face-to-face of the ethical to the state in Lévinas.[5] It has long been my habit to scavenge and tinker in the field of practical philosophy. I will conserve from Kant the discontinuity between the ethical and the political, from Lévinas the discontinuity between the ethical and the epistemological. I will suggest that the discontinuities between the ethical and the epistemological and political fields can be staged by means of the play of logic and rhetoric in fiction.[6]

Enabled by such a suggestion, I can move to another bit of prose on that page in Lévinas: 'for reasons not at all transcendental but purely logical, the object-man must figure at the beginning of all knowing'.

The figure of the 'I' as object: this representation of the holy man in Lévinas does not match our colloquial and literal expectations. My general suggestion, that the procedure of fiction can give us a simulacrum of the discontinuities inhabiting (and operating?)

the ethico-epistemic and the ethico-political, can, however, take such a figure on board. I will continue to want to say that fiction offers us an experience of the discontinuities that remain in place 'in real life'. That would be a description of fiction as an event—an indeterminate 'sharing' between writer and reader, where the effort of reading is to taste the impossible status of being figured as object in the web of the other. Reading, in this special sense, is sacred.

In this lecture I consider not only fiction as event but also fiction as task. I locate in Rabindranath Tagore (1861–1941) and J.M. Coetzee (1940–) representations of what may be read as versions of the 'I' figured as object and weave the representations together as a warning text for postcolonial political ambitions.[7] I am obviously using 'text' as 'web', coming from Latin *texere*—'to weave'.

In the second part of the chapter I move into the field of education as a nation-building calculus. I examine planning as its logic and teaching as its rhetoric—in the strong sense of figuration.

On the cover of the first *Pratichi Education Report*, there is an artwork by Rabindranath

Tagore, containing a poem, in English and Bengali, nestled in a tinted sketch, written and painted in Baghdad in 1932. Here is the poem, in Tagore's own translation:

> The night has ended.
> Put out the light of the lamp of thine own narrow corner smudged with smoke.
> The great morning which is for all appears in the East.
> Let its light reveal us to each other
> Who walk on the same path of pilgrimage.[8]

The Bengali is slightly more active: *Nikhiler alo purba akashe jolilo punyodine/Ekshathe jara cholibe tahara shokolere nik chine*. The universe's light burns in the eastern sky on this blessed day/Let those who'll walk together recognize each other. These lines resonate with what might be the mission statement of the moral entrepreneurship of the international civil society today, which, however laudable, is put together, not by democratic procedure, but largely by self-selection and networking. I am aware, of course, of the same forces at work in 'democracies'. But the presence of mechanisms of redress—electoral or constitutional—however remote, produces a faith in electoral education, which is useless if our faith is put entirely in self-selected international helpers.

'Apoman', the poem Tagore wrote more than twenty years before this, after reading Kshitimohan Sen's translations of Kabir, is much darker.[9] In this poem, Tagore uses the exact phrase 'human rights'—*manusher adhikar*—already at the beginning of the last century. What is to me more striking is that, instead of urging that human rights be immediately restored to the descendants of India's historical unfortunates, he makes a mysterious prediction, looking towards the historical future: '*apomane hote habe tahader shobar shoman*'—my unfortunate country, you will have to be equal in disgrace to each and every one of those you have disgraced millennially—a disgrace to which Kabir had responded.

How can this enigmatic sentence be understood? The idea of intertextuality, loosely defined, can be used to confront this question.

I will offer an anecdotal account of intertextuality. It will help us coast through Tagore's India, Coetzee's South Africa and the space of a tiny group of *adivasis*.[10]

In November 2002, Roald Hoffman, a Nobel Laureate chemist, gave a popular mini-lecture with slides in the basement of the Cornelia Street Café in New York. The topic was 'Movement in Constrained Spaces', by which Hoffman meant the incessant microscopic movement that goes on inside the human body to make it function. To prepare for his talk, he had asked a choreographer from neighbouring Princeton to choreograph a dance for the space of the stage, which is very small.[11] This is already intertextuality, where one text, Hoffman's, would make its point by weaving itself with another, the dance. A shot silk, as it were. Again, that venerable sense of text as in textile, and *texere* as weave.

The choreographer managed a pattern of exquisite and minute movements for two dancers, male and female, in that tiny space. But, at the back of the long and narrow bar, two singers, female and male, sang *La ci darem a mano* in full-throated ease. That wonderful aria from Mozart's *Don Giovanni*, sung with such force and skill, bought our choreographer the deep space of the bar, but also historical space—the space of an opera that has been heard and loved by millions for a few centuries. Yet her dancers gave something to Mozart as well. Full of lyric grace as a love song if heard by itself—a man telling his beloved the exquisite beauty of the place to which they will escape—*La ci darem* is, in context, a brutal seduction song of the most vicious class-fixed gendering, a gentleman seducing a confused farm girl only to fuck, and the audience sharing the joke. The two impish and acrobatic dancers on the diminutive stage, wittily partnering, gave the lie to the possibility of any such interpretation.

This is intertextuality, working both ways. Just as the chemist gave the dancer the lie, somewhat, for the movements *he* spoke of made the dance possible, so did the dancers give Mozart the lie by taking away his plot. Yet each gained something as well.

But in this case it did not work completely. Mozart is too elite for a radical New York audience. They did not catch the allusion. When the boring literary academic referred to it in a timid question, the choreographer melted in gratitude.

This *is* sometimes the task of the literary academic. To restore reference boringly in order that intertextuality may function; and to create intertextuality as well. In order to do a good job with the Tagore poem, I have to read Kabir carefully. And that will be another session with the fictive simulacrum of the helpless strength of the ethical.

J.M. Coetzee's novel *Disgrace* may be put in an intertextual relationship with Tagore's poem.[12] In representing *jare tumi niche felo she tomare bandhibe je niche*—the one you fling down will bind you down there—in rural South Africa, Coetzee offers an illustration of what that enigmatic prediction might mean: '*apomane hote hobe tahader shobar shoman*'— you will have to be equal in disgrace to all of them. Here too, intertextuality works two ways. Where Tagore alters his refrain in the last line: *mrityumajhe hobe tobe chitabhashshe shobar shoman*—you will then be equal to all of them in the ashes of death, thus predicting the death of a nation—Coetzee, writing an unsentimentally gendered narrative, makes his protagonist choose life. (I should add that Tagore's last stanza is somewhat more programmatic and asks for a call to all.)

Here is a plot summary of Coetzee's novel: David Lurie, a middle-aged male professor, sentimental consumer of metropolitan sex-work, seduces a student, and is charged with sexual harassment by the appropriate committee. He refuses to utter the formulas that will get him off. He leaves the university and goes to his possibly lesbian daughter Lucy's flower farm. The daughter is raped and beaten by two young black men and he is himself beaten and badly burnt by them. The daughter is pregnant and decides to carry the child to term. One of the rapists turns up at the neighbouring farm and is apparently a relative of the owner. This farmer Petrus, already married, proposes a concubinage style marriage to Lucy. She accepts. The English Professor starts working for an outfit that puts unwanted dogs to sleep. He has a short liaison with the unattractive married woman who runs the outfit. He writes an operetta in a desultory way. He learns to love dogs and finally learns to give up the dog that he loves to the stipulated death.

These are some of the daughter Lucy's last words in the novel. Her father is ready to send his violated daughter back to her Dutch mother. Holland is the remote metropole for the Afrikaner:

> It is as if she has not heard him. 'Go back to Petrus', she says. 'Propose the following. Say I accept his protection. Say he can put out whatever story he likes about our relationship and I won't contradict him. If he wants me to be known as his third wife, so be it.

As his concubine, ditto. But then the child becomes his too. The child becomes part of his family. As for the land, say I will sign the land over to him as long as the house remains mine. I will become a tenant on his land'....

'How humiliating', *he* says finally. ... 'yes, [she says] I agree, it is humiliating. But perhaps that is a good point to start from again....

To start at ground level. With nothing. Not with nothing but. With nothing. No cards, no weapons, no property, no rights, no dignity'.

(204–5; emphasis mine)

Apomane hote hobe tahader shobar shoman.

Insofar as *Disgrace* is a father–daughter story, the intertextuality here is with *Lear*. If Lucy ends with nothing, Cordelia in the text of *King Lear* begins with the word 'nothing'. That word signifies the withholding of speech as an instrument for indicating socially inappropriate affective value. In Cordelia's understanding, to put love in the value-form—let me measure how much—is itself absurd.

Indeed, in the first impact of the word 'nothing' in the play, this protest is mimed in the clustering of silences in the short lines among the regular iambic pentameter lines. '*Cor.* Nothing, my lord. [six syllables of silence]/ *Lear.* Nothing? [eight syllables of silence]/*Cor.*

Nothing. [eight again]/*Lear*. Nothing will come of nothing: speak again' (1.1.87–90). The metre picks up and Cordelia speaks.

Now Cordelia shows that she is also a realist and knows that love in the value-form is what makes the world go around. She is made to chide her sisters for not thinking of the love due to their husbands: 'Why have my sisters husbands if they say/They love you all?' (1.1.97–8).

Just as *Disgrace* is also a father–daughter story, so is *King Lear* also a play about dynastic succession in the absence of a son, not an unimportant topic in Jacobean England. It has been abundantly pointed out that the play's turnaround can be measured by the fact that 'the presence of Cordelia at the head of a French army … marks the final horrific stage in the process by which Lear's division of the kingdom goes on turning the world upside down'.[13] Thus the love due to fathers bows to the love due to husbands and is then displaced, as it were. It is this story of fathers and husbands, and dynastic succession at the very inception of capitalist colonialism that *Disgrace* destabilizes, re-asking the question of the Enlightenment ('let those who will walk together get to know each other by the dawning universal *light'*, says the cover of the *Pratichi Report*) with reference to the public sphere and the classed and gendered subject, when Lucy, 'perhaps' a lesbian, decides to carry the child of rape to term and agrees to 'marry' Petrus, who is not (one of) the biological father(s).

Lucy's 'nothing' is the same word but carries a different meaning from Cordelia's. It is not the withholding of speech protesting the casting of love in the value form *and* giving it the wrong value. It is rather the casting aside of the affective value system attached to reproductive heteronormativity as it is accepted as the currency to measure human dignity. I do not think this is an acceptance of rape, but a refusal to be raped by instrumentalizing reproduction. Coetzee's Lucy is made to make clear that the 'nothing' is not to be itself measured as the absence of 'everything' by the old epistemico-affective value form—the system of knowing-loving. It is not 'nothing but', Lucy insists. It is an originary 'nothing', a scary beginning. Why should we imagine that centuries of malpractice—*shotek shatabdir ashommanbhar*—can be conveniently undone by diversified committees, such as the one that 'tried' David Lurie for rape Enlightenment-style?[14]

'Unaccommodated man is no more but such a poor, bare, forked animal as thou art', Lear had said to Edgar's faked madness, erasing the place of the phallus: 'a poor, bare, *forked* animal'. What does it mean, in the detritus of colonialism, for one from the ruling race to call for interpellation as 'unaccommodated woman, a poor, bare, forked animal', and hold negotiating power without sentimentality in that very forkèdness? What if Lévinas's catachrestic holy man is a catachrestic holy woman, quite unlike the maternity that Lévinas embarrassingly places in the stomach in the passage from which I quoted? Is it a gendered special case, or can it claim generality, as making visible the difficulty of the postcolonial formula: a new nation. Neither *Lear* nor *Disgrace* is a blueprint for unmediated social policy. These are figures, asking for disfiguration, as figures must. And it is the representation of the 'I' as figured object—as woman relinquishing the child as property, as always, *and* as former colonizer in the ex-colony. This is how critique is operated through fictions.

I emphasize that it is not an equality in death—*mrityumajhe*. It is not the sort of equality that suicide bombing may bring. Suicidal resistance is a message inscribed in the body when no other means will get through. It is both execution and mourning, for both self and other, where you die with me for the same cause, no matter which side you are on, with the implication that there is no dishonour in such shared and innocent death. That is an equality in disgrace brought about by the withholding of response, or a 'response' so disingenuously requiring duress as to be no response at all, as from Israel to Palestine.[15]

If Lucy is intertextual with *Lear*, Lurie is intertextual with Kafka's *The Trial*, a novel not about beginning with nothing, but ending like a dog when civil society crumbles.[16] Here is the end of *The Trial*, where Josef K.'s well-organized civil society gives way:

> Logic is no doubt unshakable, but it can't withstand a person who wants to live. Where was the judge he'd never seen? Where was the high court he'd ever reached? He raised his hands and spread out all his fingers. But the hands of one man were right at K.'s throat, while the other thrust the knife into his heart and turned it there twice. With failing sight K. saw how the men drew near his face, leaning cheek-to-cheek to observe the verdict. 'Like a dog!' he said; it seemed as though the shame was to outlive him.

This is how Lurie understands Lucy's remarks about 'nothing but'. Not as a beginning in disgraceful equality but as the end of civil society (with the withdrawal of the colonizer?), where only shame is guaranteed continuity. This is a profound but typical misunderstanding. And this brings me to the second point about literature. The literary text gives rhetorical signals to the reader, which leads to activating the readerly imagination. Literature advocates in this special way. These are not the ways of expository prose. Literary reading has to be learned. Metaphor leans on concept and concept on metaphor, logic nestles in rhetoric, but they are not the same and one cannot be effaced in the other. If the social sciences describe the rules of the game, literary reading teaches how to play. One cannot be effaced in the other. This is too neat an opposition, of course. But for the moment, let it suffice as a rule of thumb.

What rhetorical signal does *Disgrace* give to the canny reader? It comes through the use of focalization, described by Mieke Bal as 'the relation between the vision and that which is "seen"'.[17] This term is deemed more useful than 'point of view' or 'perspective' because it emphasizes the fluidity of narrative—the impression of (con)sequence as well as the transactional nature of reading.

Disgrace is relentless in keeping the focalization confined to David Lurie. Indeed, this is the vehicle of the sympathetic portrayal of David Lurie. When Lucy is resolutely denied focalization, the reader is provoked, for he or she does not want to share in Lurie-the-chief-focalizer's inability to 'read' Lucy as patient and agent. No reader is content with acting out the failure of reading. This is the rhetorical signal to the active reader, to counterfocalize. This shuttle between focalization and the making of an alternative narrative as the reader's running commentary, as it were, used to be designated by the prim phrase 'dramatic irony' when I was an undergraduate. You will see immediately how much more effortful and active this counterfocalization is than what that older term can indicate. This provocation into counterfocalization is the 'political' in political fiction—the transformation of a tendency into a crisis.[18]

When Lurie asks, after Lucy's impassioned speech, 'Like a dog?' Lucy simply agrees, 'Yes, like a dog'. She does not provide the explanation that the reader who can work the intertextuality will provide. *Lear* and

The Trial are not esoteric texts. We can sense the deep contradiction of a split understanding of postcoloniality here: between the risk of beginning with nothing and the breakdown of civil societies. If not, we can at least see that Lurie literalizes her remark and learns to love dogs as the other of being-human, as a source, even, of ethical lessons of a special sort. He is staged as unable to touch either the racial or the gendered other. These may be Lucy's last words, but the novel continues, focalizing Lurie loving dogs, avoiding bathos only by his obvious race-gender illiteracy, as we counterfocalize the absent Lucy.

Literary reading teaches us to learn from the singular and the unverifiable. It is not that literary reading does not generalize. It is just that those generalizations are not on evidentiary ground. In this area, what is known is proved by *vyavahara*, or setting-to-work. Martin Luther King, in his celebrated speech 'Beyond Vietnam', given on 4 April 1967 in Riverside Church[19] had tried to imagine the other again and again. In his own words, '[p]erhaps the more difficult but no less necessary task is to speak for those who have been designated as our enemies.... Surely we must understand their feelings even if we do not condone their actions'.

Here is a setting-to-work of what in the secular imagination is the literary impulse: to imagine the other who does not resemble the self. King, being a priest, had put it in terms of liberation theology, in the name of 'the one who loved his enemies so fully that he died for them'. For the secular imagination, that transcendental narrative is just that, a narrative, singular and unverifiable. When it is set to work, it enters the arena of the probable: King's imagination of the Viet Cong. I believe this is why Aristotle said *poiesis* or making-in-fiction was *philosophoteron*—a better instrument of knowledge—than *historia*—because it allowed us to produce the probable rather than account for that which has been possible.

In my words on suicide bombing, I was trying to follow Dr King's lead halfway, use the secular imagination as emancipatory instrument. When I was a graduate student, on the eve of the Vietnam War, I lived in the same house as Paul Wolfowitz, the ferocious Deputy Secretary of Defense who was the chief talking head for the war on Iraq. He was a Political Science undergraduate, disciple of Allan Bloom, the conservative political philosopher. As I have watched him on television lately, I have often thought that if he had had serious training in literary reading and/or the imagining of the enemy as human, his position on Iraq would not be so inflexible. This is not a verifiable conviction; but it is in view of such hopes that humanities teaching acts itself out.

To repeat: literature is not verifiable. The only way a reading establishes itself—without guarantees—is by sharing the steps of the reading. That is the experience of the impossible, ethical discontinuity shaken up in a simulacrum. Unless you take a step with me, there will be no interdisciplinarity, only the tedium of turf battles.

Insofar as Lucy is a figure that makes visible the rational kernel of the institution of marriage—rape, social security, property, human continuity—we can check her out with Herculine Barbin, the nineteenth-century hermaphrodite who committed suicide but left a memoir, which Foucault edited and made available.

Herculine Barbin was a scholar—a diligent student who became a schoolmistress. But when she was named a man by doctors, she could not access the scholarly position—of writing and speaking to a general public—that

Kant secures for the enlightened subject in 'What is Enlightenment?'[20]

Let us look at Herculine/Abel's cautious elation at the moment of entry into the world of men:

> So, it was done [*C'en était donc fait*]. Civil status called me to belong henceforth to that half of the human race that is called the strong sex [*L'état civil m'appelait à faire partie désormais de cette moitié du genre humain, appelé le sexe fort*]. I, who had been raised until the age of twenty-one in religious houses, among shy [*timides*] female companions, was going to leave behind me a past entirely delightful [*tout un passé délicieux*], like Achilles, and enter the lists, armed with my weakness alone and my profound inexperience of men and things![21]

It is this hope—of entering the public sphere as the felicitous subject—that is dashed as the possibility of agency is annulled in suicide (98).

Barbin cannot articulate the relationship between the denial of agency and the incapability to reproduce. Yet, Tiresias-like, he offers a critical account of marriage:

> It has been given to me, as a man, the most intimate and deep knowledge of all the aptitudes, all the secrets, of the female

character. I read in that heart, as in an open book. I count every beat of it. In a word, I have the secret of its strength and the measure of its weakness; and just for that reason I would make a detestable husband; I also feel that all my joys would be poisoned in marriage and that I would cruelly abuse, perhaps, the immense advantage that would be mine, an advantage that would turn against me. (107; translation modified)

I presented 'Can the Subaltern Speak?' as a paper over twenty-five years ago. In that paper I suggested that the subaltern could not 'speak' because, in the absence of institutionally validated agency, there was no listening subject. My listening, separated by space and time, was perhaps an ethical impulse. But I am with Kant in thinking that such impulses do not lead to the political. There must be a presumed collectivity of listening and countersigning subjects and agents in the public sphere for the subaltern to 'speak'. Herculine Barbin wrote abundantly, presuming a reader repeatedly. And yet she could not speak. Her solution would be the normalization of the multi-sexed subject, a civil and agential rather than subjective solution. There would then be a listening public who could countersign her 'speech act'.

In the arrangement of counterfocalization within the validating institution of the novel in English, the second half of *Disgrace* makes the subaltern speak, but does not presume to give 'voice', either to Petrus or Lucy. This is not the novel's failure, but rather a politically fastidious awareness of the limits of its power. By the general dramatically ironic presentation of Lurie, he is shown to 'understand' Petrus by the neat reversal of the master–slave dialectic without sublation: 'Petrus needs him not for pipefitting or plumbing but to hold things, to pass him tools—to be his *handlanger*, in fact. The role is not one he objects to. Petrus is a good workman, it is an education to watch him. It is Petrus himself that he is beginning to dislike' (136–7). Once again, the novel and Lurie part company, precisely on the issue of reading, of control. This is a perfectly valid reading, as is the invocation of the end of Kafka's *The Trial* to describe the difficult birth of the new nation. And it is precisely this limited perfect validity of the liberal white ex-colonizer's understanding that *Disgrace* questions through the invitation to focalize the enigma of Lucy. Petrus's one-liner on Lucy shows more kinship with the novel's verdict: 'She is a forward-looking lady, not backward-looking' (136). If we, like Lurie, ignore the enigma of Lucy, the novel, being fully focalized precisely by Lurie, can be made to say every racist thing.[22] Postcoloniality from below can then be reduced to the education of Pollux, the young rapist who is related to Petrus. Counterfocalized, it can be acknowledged as perhaps the first moment in Lucy's refusal of rape by generalizing it into all heteronormative sexual practice: '"When it comes to men and sex, David, nothing surprises me any more…. They spur each other on…." "And the third one, the boy?" "He was there to learn"' (158–9). The incipient bathos of Lurie's literalism ('like a dog' means love dogs; forgiveness from Melanie's parents means prostrating himself on the floor before them (173); loving dogs means letting one of them into the operetta (215); even the possibility that the last Christian scene of man giving up dog may slide into a rictus,[23] given the overarching narrative context) can be seen, in a reading that ignores the function of Lucy in the narrative, as the novel's failure, rather than part of its rhetorical web.

I want now to come to the second way in which Tagore's refrain can be understood: the failure of democracy.

The Pratichi Trust in India,[24] to whose *Report* I have referred above, is doing astute work because it realizes that, if the largest sector of the electorate misses out on early education, democracy cannot function, for it then allows the worst of the upper sectors to flourish. Democracy sinks to that level and we are all equal in disgrace. When we read statistics on who wins and who loses the elections, the non-specialist located middle-class as well as the rest of the world, if it cares, thinks it shows how the country thinks. No. In the largest and lowest sector of the electorate, there is a considerable supply of affect, good and bad; there is native sharpness and there is acquired cunning. But there is no rational choice. Election does not even pretend to be based on rational platforms. (This applies to the United States as well, in another way. But it would take me too far to develop that here.) Gendering must be understood simply here: female teachers are preferred, though they have less authority; gendering presuppositions must be changed through education, and so on.

There is little I can add to the Trust's magisterial work. After a general caution, that work in this sphere runs the risk of structural atrophy, like diversified committees in *Disgrace*, and therefore must be interrupted by the ethical, I will add a few codicils here and there.

Professor Amartya Sen, the founder of the Trust, supports the state in opposing 'the artificially generated need for private tuition', artificial because generated by careless non-teaching in the free primary schools.[25] While the state waits to implement this opposition legally, I have been trying to provide free collective 'private tuition' to supplement the defunct primary schools, to a tiny sector of the most disenfranchised. It is my hope that private tuition in this form can be nationalized and thus lose its definition. I will ask some questions in conclusion, which will make the direction of my thoughts clear. The one-on-one of 'private' tuition—at the moment in the service of rote learning that cannot relate to the nurturing of the ethical impulse—is the only way to undo the abdication of the politically planned 'public' education. 'Private tuition', therefore, is a relation to transform rather than prohibit. The tutorial system at the other end of the spectrum—the prestigious institutions of tertiary education in the Euro-US—is proof of this.

I must repeat that I am enthralled by the report and whatever I am adding is in the nature of a supplement from a literary person. The work of the Trust is largely structural. The humanities—training in literary reading in particular—is good at textural change. Each discipline has its own species of 'setting to work'—and the texture of the imagination belongs to the teacher of literary reading. All good work is imaginative, of course. But the humanities have little else.

There is a tiny exchange on page 69 of the book: 'On the day of our visit [to a school in Medinipur], we interviewed four children of Class 4 ... Well, can you tell us something about what was taught? All four children were silent'.

Part of the silence rises from the very class apartheid that bad rural education perpetuates.[26] The relationship between the itinerant inspector and the child is, in addition, hardly ethical.

Training in literary reading can prepare one to work at these silences. I will submit an example which would be useless to translate here. It is lesson 5 from *Amader Itihash*, a Class 4 history book, specifically devoted to national liberation: one item, which is the story of Nelson Mandela. Let us overlook the implicit misrepresentation of Gandhi's role in Mandela's political victory in the lifting of apartheid, or the suggestive detail that the section on national liberation starts with George Washington. One cannot, however, overlook, if one is a reader of Bengali, the hopeless ornamentation of the prose, incomprehensible to teacher and student alike at the subaltern level, in the outer reaches of rural West Bengal. The point is not only to ask for 'a radically enhanced set of commitments' 'from the primary teachers', as the *Report* stresses. The real disgrace of rural primary education is that even the *good* teacher, with the best will in the world, has been so indoctrinated into rote learning that, even if s/he could understand the lugubrious prose and even if s/he had retained or imbibed enough general knowledge of the world—both doubtful propositions—the technique of emphasizing meaning is not what s/he would understand by teaching. Elsewhere I have emphasized this as the systematic difference in teaching between *baralok* and *chhotolok*—translated by Pratichi as high-born and low-born, brave attempts—*gatar khatano* and *matha khatano*—manual labour and intellectual labour does not quite translate the active sense of *khatano*—setting to work, then, of the body alone, and not of the mind as well—that keeps class apartheid alive.

The common sight of a child of the rural poor trying to make the head engage in answer to a textbook question and failing is as vivid a figure of withholding humanity as anything in Tagore or Coetzee. The 'silence' is active with pain and resentment.

The solution is not to write new textbooks, the liberal intellectuals' favourite option. The teachers at this level do not know how to use a book, any book, however progressive. Many of the textbooks, for instance, have a list of pedagogic goals at the top of each lesson. The language of these lists is abstract, starting with the title: *shamortho*, capacity. Sometimes, for nine or ten lessons in a row, this abstract title is followed by the remark: 'see previous lesson'. No primary or non-formal teacher over the last 23 years has ever noticed this in my presence, and, when informed of the presence of this pedagogic machinery, been able to understand it, let alone implement it. Given the axiomatics of the so-called education within which the teacher has received what goes for training, it is foolish to expect implementation.

There are progressive textbooks that try to combine Bengali and arithmetic—the famous *Kajer Pata*. This combination causes nothing but confusion in student and teacher alike on this level. And frankly, it serves no specific purpose here. There are also books where some metropolitan liberal or a committee of them tries to engage what they think is a rural audience. I wish I had the time to recount the failure of their imagination case by case. There is no possibility of the emergence of the ethical when the writing subject's sense of superiority is rock solid. The useless coyness of these failed attempts would be amusing if the problem were not so disgraceful. Both Hindu and Muslim poets are included—communalism must be avoided at all costs, of course. The point is lost on these children—though a sort of equality is achieved. All poetry is equally opaque, occasions for memorization without comprehension, learning two-way meanings— what does a mean? b; and what is b? a, of course. The meaning of meaning is itself compromised for these children, these teachers. A new textbook drowns in that compromise.

Two girls, between eleven and fifteen years of age, show me what they are being taught in primary school. It is the piece about South Africa. I ask them some questions. They have absolutely no clue at all what the piece is about, as they don't about any piece in the book, about any piece in any book. To say 'they haven't understood this piece' would be to grant too much. The girls are not unintelligent. Indeed, one of them is, I think, strikingly intelligent. They tell me their teachers would go over the material again the next day.

The next day after school, we meet again. Did the teachers explain? 'Reading *poriyechhe*', is the answer—an untranslatable Bengali phrase for which there are equivalents in all the major Indian languages, no doubt. 'They made us read reading' would perhaps convey the absurdity? Any piece is a collection of discrete spelling exercises to be read in a high drone with little regard to punctuation. The scandal is that everyone knows this. It is embarrassing to put it in a writing about Tagore and Coetzee. It is better to present social scientific surveys in English. This too is a way of disgracing the disenfranchised.

To continue with the narrative: after the girls' answer begins the process of explaining. As I have already mentioned, the experience of a head attempting but failing to set itself to work is killingly painful. Most of us interrupt such silences with noise, speak up and create a version of explanation to break the experience. At that point we think we are teaching although no teaching is taking place. Sometimes we learn to resist this by excruciating self-control that often fails.

In *Foe*, another novel by J.M. Coetzee, there is a moment when a character called Friday (as in Robinson Crusoe), an abducted savage with his tongue cut out, resists the attempt of the white woman to teach him how to write.[27] Varieties of such resistance in the ground-level rural classroom can be read as the anger of the intelligent child not being able to work his or her head. Such readings are necessarily off the mark. But the literary critic is practised in learning from the unverifiable.

If the older girl was just frustrated by not grasping at all what I was trying to explain, the younger one, the strikingly intelligent one, faced me with that inexorably closed look, jaws firmly set, that reminds one of Friday, withholding. No response to repeated careful questions going over the same ground over and over again, simplifying the story of Nelson Mandela further at every go. These are students who have no concept or percept of the neighbouring districts, of their own state of West Bengal—because, as the *Pratichi Report* points out, they have arrived at Class 4 through neglect and no teaching. How will they catch the reference to Africa?

Into the second hour, sitting on the floor in that darkening room, I tried another tack. Forget Africa, try *shoman adhikar*—equal rights. It was impossible to explain rights in a place with no plumbing, pavement, electricity, stores, without doors and windows. Incidentally, do people really check—rather than interrupt the painful experience of having failed to teach—the long-term residue of so-called legal awareness seminars? What is learnt through repeated brushes with the usual brutality of the rural judiciary is not significantly changed by the conviction that the benevolent among the masters will help them litigate. What is it to develop the subject—the capital I—of human rights, rather than a feudal dispensation of human rights breeding dependency and litigious blackmail and provoking a trail of vendetta in those punishers punished remotely? Let us return to the schoolroom in gathering dusk.

It is common sense that children have short attention spans. I was so helpless in my inability to explain that I was tyrannizing the girls. At the time it seemed as if we were locked together in an effort to let response emerge and blossom with its own energy. The ethical as task rather than event is effortful. And perhaps an hour and a half into the struggle, I put my hand next to the bright one's purple-black hand to explain apartheid. Next to that rich colour, this pasty brown hand seemed white. And to explain *shoman adhikar*, equal rights, Mandela's demand, a desperate formula presented itself to me: *ami ja, tumi ta*—what I, that you. Remember this is a student, not an asylum seeker in the metropole, in whose name many millions of dollars are moved around even as we speak.[28] This is just two students, accepting oppression as normality, understanding their designated textbook.

Response did emerge. Yesses and noes were now given; even, if I remember right, a few words uttered as answers to questions. In a bit I let them go.

The next morning I asked them to set down what they remembered of the previous day's lesson. The older one could call up nothing. The younger one, the more intelligent one, produced this: '*ami ja, tumi ta, raja here gachhe*'—what I, that you, the king was defeated. A tremendous achievement in context but, if one thinks of all the children studying under the West Bengal Board, including the best students from the best schools in Kolkata, with whom these girls are competing, this is a negligible result.

I have no doubt that even this pitiful residue of the content of the lesson is now long lost and forgotten.

The incident took place about 10 years ago. The two girls would have been young women now, in high school. Speaking to them and their teachers in December, I stressed repeatedly the importance of explaining the text, of explaining repeatedly, of checking to see if the student has understood. A futile exercise. You do not teach how to play a game by talking about it. No one can produce meanings of unknown words. There are no dictionaries, and, more important, no habit of consulting dictionaries.

As I continued with the useless harangue, I said, 'As two of you might remember, I spent two hours explaining Nelson Mandela to you some years ago. It is important to explain.' A fleeting smile, no eye contact, passed across the face of the bright one, sitting in the last row. It is unusual for such signals to pass from her class to mine.[29]

The number of calculative moves to be made and sustained in the political sphere, with the deflecting and overdetermined calculus of the vicissitudes of gendered class-mobility factored in at every stop, in order for the irony-shared-from-below communication to be sustained at this level, would require immense systemic change. Yet, in the supplementary relationship between the possibility of that fleeting smile—a sign of the interruptive emergence of the ethical—and the daunting labour of the political calculus, we must begin with the end, which must remain the possibility of the ethical. That inconvenient effort is the uncertain ground of every just society. If the political calculus becomes the means *and* the end, justice is ill served and no change will stick. The peculiar thing about gendering is that, in Lucy's vision of 'starting with nothing', in the reproductive situation shorn of the fetishization of property, in the child given up as body's product, the ethical moment can perhaps emerge—at least so the fiction says.[30]

I have recounted this narrative to make clear that although on the literary register, the register of the singular and the unverifiable (this story, for example, is unverifiable because you have nothing but my testimony), the suggestive smile, directed by indirection and a shared experience, is a good event; it has no significance in terms of the public sphere, to which education should give access. The discontinuity between the ethical and the political is here instrumentalized—between the rhetoric of pedagogy and the logic of its fruition in the public sphere. For the smile of complicity to pass between the *adivasi* and the caste-Indian, unprovoked, marks an immense advance. But it is neither a beginning nor an end, only an irreducible grounding condition.

When I was attempting to teach in that darkening room, I had no thought but to get through. It so happened that the topic was *shoman adhikar*, equal rights. Writing this for you, on the other hand, I put myself grandiosely in Tagore's poem: *manusher odhikare bonchito korechho jaare, shommukhe danraye rekhe tobu kole dao nai sthan*—those whom you have deprived of human rights, whom you have kept standing face-to-face and yet not taken in your arms. So, spending considerable skill and labour, to teach precisely the meaning of *shoman adhikar*, was I perhaps undoing the poet's description of the behaviour of the Hindu historical dominant, denying human rights over centuries to the outcastes (today's *dalit*s) and *adivasi*s? The point I am laboriously making is that it is not so. Although the literary mode of instruction activates the subject, the capital I, in order to be secured it must enter the political calculus of the public sphere. Private voluntarism such as mine remains a mongrel practice between the literary and the rational, rhetoric and logic.

And so the reader of literature asks the social scientists a question. Is it not possible for the globally beleaguered state to institute civil service positions that will call, on a regular and optional basis, upon interested humanities professionals from the highest ranks to train ground-level teachers, periodically, yet with some continuity, gradually integrating and transforming the existing training structure, thus to deconstruct or sublate private tuition and slowly make it less possible for 'a teacher of [*sic*] Birbhum village' to say: 'How can we carry over the training to our classrooms? *Baro baro katha bala soja*—Talking big is easy'.[31]

Before I had started thinking about the heritage of 'disgrace', I had tried to initiate the production of same-language dictionaries in the major Indian languages, specifically for ground-level teachers and students. It came to nothing, because the situation was not imaginable by those whom I had approached, and because the NRI (non-resident Indian, Indian designation for diasporics) has other kinds of uses. Should the NRI have no role but to help place the state in metropolitan economic bondage? Is it not possible to think of subaltern single-language dictionaries as an important step towards fostering the habit of freedom—the habit of finding a meaning for oneself whoever suggests this? Is it not possible to think, not of writing new textbooks, but of revising what is now in existence—to make them more user-friendly for the least privileged, even as such teachers and students are texturally engaged? I do not believe the more privileged child would suffer from such a change, though I can foresee a major outcry. It must be repeated, to foster such freedom is simply to work at freedom in the sphere of necessity, otherwise ravaged by the ravages of political economy—no more than 'the grounding condition [*Grundbedingung*] for the true realm of freedom', always around the corner.[32]

Shakespeare, Kafka, Tagore, Coetzee, Amartya Sen. Heavy hitters. My questions are banal. I am always energized by that paragraph in the third volume of *Capital* from which I quote above, and where Marx writes, in a high philosophical tone: 'The true realm of freedom, the development of human powers as an end in itself begins beyond [the realm of necessity], though it can only flourish with this realm of necessity as its ground.' That sentence is followed by this one: 'The reduction of the working day is its grounding condition.' In Marx's text, philosophy must thus displace itself into the everyday struggle. In my argument, literature, insofar as it is in the service of the emergence of the critical, must also displace itself thus. Its task is to foster yet another displacement: into a work for the remote possibility of the precarious production of an infrastructure that can in turn produce a Lucy or her focalizer, figuring forth an equality that takes disgrace in its stride.

Notes and References

1. This essay was first presented as a Deuskar Lecture at the Centre for Studies in Social Sciences, Calcutta, on 10 February 2003 and was published in *Diacritics*, Vol. 32, no. 3–4 (December 2002).

2. Jacques Derrida, *Adieu to Emmanuel Lévinas*, tr. Pascale-Anne Brault and Michael Naas (Stanford: Stanford University Press, 1999), pp. 51–9.

3. Emmanuel Lévinas, *Otherwise than Being: Or Beyond Essence*, tr. Alphonso Lingis (Pittsburgh: Duquesne University Press, 1981), p. 58; translation modified.

4. Derrida 1999, p. 59; translation modified. There is a footnote in the text to Paul Ricoeur's *Conflict of Interpretations*, tr. Don Ihde (Evanston:

Northwestern University Press, 1974), p. 99. The next quoted passage is from the same page.

5. See Derrida 1999, pp. 29–33, for a discussion of this.

6. I first learned to notice this from Derrida's article 'White Mythology' whose subtitle is 'Metaphor in the Text of Philosophy' (*Margins of Philosophy*, tr. Alan Bass, Chicago: University of Chicago Press, 1982), pp. 209–71.

7. This paper was the first Deuskar lecture at the Centre for Studies in Social Sciences, Calcutta, in Kolkata, India. In the second lecture of the series, I offered a reading of Salman Rushdie's *Midnight's Children* as a President Schreber-style critique of postcolonial political ambitions.

8. Pratichi (India) Trust, *The Pratichi Education Report*, Introduction, Amartya Sen (Delhi: TLM Books, 2002).

9. Kabir, *Songs of Kabir*, tr. Rabindranath Tagore from Kshitimohan Sen (New York: Macmillan, 1915).

10. *Adivasi* is the name used commonly for so-called Indian 'tribals', by general account the inhabitants of India at the time of the arrival of Indo-European speakers in the second millennium BC.

11. Diann Sichel, 'Mass, Momentum and Energy Transport (Living Space)', Dancers: Josiah Pearsall, Melanie Velo-Simpson, Singers: Wendy Baker, Erik Kroncke.

12. J.M. Coetzee, *Disgrace* (New York: Viking, 2000).

13. William Shakespeare, *King Lear* (Cambridge, MA: Harvard University Press, 1959), Arden Edition, p. 141.

14. For an analysis of this rhetorical question, see Rosalind C. Morris, 'The Mute and the Unspeakable: Political Subjectivity, Violent Crime, and "the Sexual Thing" in a South African Mining Community', in *Law and Disorder in the Postcolony*, ed. Jean and John Comaroff (Chicago: University of Chicago Press, 2006), pp. 57–101.

15. Since 1983, when I delivered 'Can the Subaltern Speak?' as a lecture at the Summer Institute at the University of Illinois in Champaign-Urbana, I have been interested in suicide as envoi. Partha Chatterjee reminded me in conversation (31 October 2003) that the 'cause' is metaleptically constructed by the suicide, as the effect of an 'effect'. My point is that Lucy is not represented as the 'subject' of a 'cause'. Her representation may be read as Lévinas's object-human as the figure that subtends all knowing, including the cognition of a cause. About suicide bombing I speculate at greater length in 'Terror: A Speech After 9/11', *Boundary*, 2, 31.2 (2004): 81–111; reprinted in Italian translation in *aut aut* 329 (January/March 2006), pp. 6–46.

16. Franz Kafka, *The Trial*, tr. Breon Mitchell (New York: Schocken Books, 1998). The quoted passage is from page 231.

17. Mieke Bal, *Narratology: Introduction to the Theory of Narrative* (Toronto: University of Toronto Press, 1985), p. 100.

18. Karl Marx uses this to describe why the tendency of the rate of profit to fall does not result in increasingly lower profits (*Capital: A Critique of Political Economy*, tr. David Fernbach, New York: Vintage, 1981, vol. 3, pp. 365–6 *passim*).

19. *Black Protest: History, Documents and Analyses, 1619 to the Present* (ed.), Joanne Grant, 2nd edn, Greenwich, CT: Fawcett, 1974, pp. 418–25.

20. Immanuel Kant, 'An Answer to the Question: What is Enlightenment', in *Practical Philosophy*, tr. and ed. Mary J. Gregor (Cambridge, UK: Cambridge University Press, 1996).

21. *Herculine Barbin: Being the Recently Discovered Memoirs of a Nineteenth-Century French Hermaphrodite* [no tr. given] (New York: Pantheon, 1980), p. 89, translation modified.

22. For a debate over such readings, see Peter D. McDonald, '*Disgrace* Effects', and David Attwell, 'Race in *Disgrace*', in *Interventions* 4.3 (2002): 321–41.

23. This possibility of an uneasy snigger (as well as the 'giving up' at the end of Coetzee's novel)

may mark something irreducible, the seeming 'abyss'—we think also of the incessant back-and-forth of the abyssal—between the 'I' of the 'I think' and the presumed self-identity of the animal: 'This automotricity as auto-affection and self-relation, before the discursive thematic of a statement or an *ego cogito*, indeed of a *cogito ergo sum*, is the character recognized in the living and in animality in general. But between that self-relationship (that Self, that *ipseity*) and the *I* of the "I think" there is, it seems, an abyss' (Derrida, 'L'animal que donc je suis [à suivre], in *L'animal autobiographique*, ed. Marie-Louise Mallet, Paris: Galilée, 1999, p. 300). It is possible that the dull effort of a cogitative Lurie has an abyssality that must not be forgotten as we attempt to acknowledge the enigmatic historiality of the mixed-race postcolonial child of rape deliberately given up as property for the adopted father, Black Christian, a Petrus upon which rock the future, guaranteeing tenancy for the colonial turned native, is founded. It is not the object-human as a figure with nothing that comes before all else, but the look of the naked animot (a word that the reader must learn from the essay by Derrida I have already cited; a word [*mot*] that marks the irreducible heterogeneity of animality). This is Derrida's critique of Lévinas. I have often felt that the formal logic of Coetzee's fiction mimes ethical moves in an uncanny way. The (non)relationship between the cogitation of animality and the setting-to-work of gendered postcolonialism in *Disgrace* may be such an uncanny miming. The 'dull decrepitude' of the former is where equality in disgrace is impossible, we cannot disgrace the animot. It is the limit of *apomane hote habe tahader shobar shoman*; and to call it a limit is to speak from one side. Since my ethical texts are Kant, Lévinas, Derrida, and my fictions are 'Apoman' (Tagore, *Gitanjali*, tr. Joe Winters, Kolkata: Writers' Workshop, 1998, pp. 140–1), *Disgrace*, and the uncoercive rearrangement of desire, I have not considered J. M. Coetzee's staged speculations about animality and the human in 'Lives of Animals' (in *The Lives of Animals*, ed. Amy Gutmann, Princeton: Princeton University Press, 1999).

24. The Pratichi (India) Trust and the Pratichi Institute work for greater equity and efficiency in the areas of education and health, with a special emphasis on gender equality. The organizations work primarily in West Bengal, but also in Jharkhand, Orissa, and the North East of India.

25. *Pratichi Education Report*, p. 10.

26. I have developed the idea of the role of rural education in maintaining class apartheid in 'Righting Wrongs', in *Other Asias* (Boston: Blackwell, 2008).

27. J.M. Coetzee, *Foe* (New York: Penguin, 1986).

28. Clyde Prestowitz, *Rogue Nation: American Unilateralism and the Failure of Good Intentions* (New York: Basic Books, 2003) argues that the US wants to make everyone American and there left and right meet. The same, I think, can now be said of Europe. This is too big a topic to develop here. What I urge in the text is the need to imagine a world that is not necessarily looking for help.

29. She died in 2003 of encephalitis. Her name was Shamoli Sabar. She is memorialized in figure— of my 'Righting Wrongs' (in *Human Rights, Human Wrongs*, ed. Nicholas Owen, Oxford: Oxford University Press, 2003). She was one of the signatories of the petition. I offer this essay to her memory.

30. We have to have an idea of how fiction can be made to speak through the transactional heading beyond the limits of the author's authority, which would expose the frivolousness of a position such as Rajat Ray's in *Exploring Emotional History: Gender, Mentality, and Literature in the Indian Awakening* (New Delhi: Oxford University Press, 2001), pp. 79, 115n28.

31. *Pratichi Education Report*, p. 68.

32. Karl Marx, *Capital*, vol. 3, tr. David Fernbach (New York: Vintage, 1981), p. 959.

Index